Contents

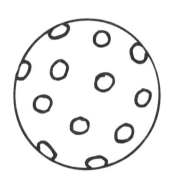

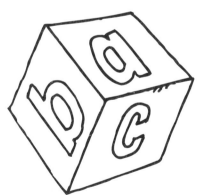

GW00384303

Introduction

Developing social skills

Developing appropriate social skills is essential for all young children if they are to succeed in other aspects of their learning and become confident members of society. They need to feel positive about themselves and at ease as they interact with those around them. This interaction is underpinned by the child's ability to form good relationships with the adults and children with whom they share their daily lives. Children need to feel comfortable and secure in different group situations and to realize that their personal contributions are valuable. Equally, they should be at ease as they work alone, know where to access what they need, and feel confident to make their own choices. It is important that children respect their own needs, views and feelings and understand that the needs, views and feelings of others might not necessarily be the same. Becoming aware of their own culture and community helps children to develop a positive self-image and sense of belonging, while learning about the cultures and communities of others encourages understanding of and respect for these.

The Early Learning Goals

The Early Learning Goals for Personal, social and emotional development set out in the QCA's document *Curriculum guidance for the foundation stage* are divided into six separate clusters and the activities in this book focus on five of these clusters. Children's dispositions and attitudes are enhanced by ensuring that activities are based on what they are interested in and understand. They are encouraged to try new activities, suggest ideas and speak in front of a group, and there are opportunities to develop concentration skills. Self-confidence and self-esteem are enhanced as children express their own feelings by, for example, using simple finger puppets.

Making relationships is given the greatest emphasis in this book. The important skills of sharing and turn-taking are developed gradually over several activities while working as part of a group. Following simple rules and forming friendships have separate activities focusing specifically on these skills. The children are asked to consider the consequences of their actions and the difference between right and wrong as they take part in activities related to behaviour and self-control, and they develop a sense of

community as they think about caring for the nursery environment. The Early Learning Goals for the sixth cluster, self-care, will be covered automatically as the children select the resources that they need for the activities, work independently and look after their own personal hygiene, such as washing their hands.

The ideas suggested in this book can be applied equally well to the documents on pre-school education published for Scotland, Wales and Northern Ireland.

Baseline Assessment

The activities are focused around developing skills in young children that will enable them to achieve the Early Learning Goals for Personal, social and emotional development during the Foundation Stage. This will allow them to confidently tackle the Baseline Assessment tasks that they will be expected to complete as they enter Reception in mainstream school.

How to use this book

This book aims to show how you can introduce and develop social skills with young children. Each activity concentrates on a new skill or a progressively advanced level of a skill previously introduced and practised.

The activities are designed to be used according to the children's level of development. Suggestions are given to simplify the activities for younger or less able children and extend them for those who are older or more able. The photocopiable sheets are not intended to be used in isolation but as a continuation of a practical task. The photocopiable sheet that accompanies each task aims to consolidate learning and also provides a record of each child's individual achievement. Where the child is required to write on the sheet it is described as an 'Individual recording' and can be kept for assessment purposes, otherwise it is referred to as an 'Individual task'.

All of the activities require the presence and interaction of an adult. It is important therefore that the activities are incorporated into planning and that the adult leading the activity is fully prepared and aware of the purpose and learning objective of each activity. On page 32, you will find a 'Skills development chart'. This shows a clear progression of the skills that the children will be developing as they complete the activities in the book.

Progression

Many of the activities in the book have been devised to ensure a gradual progression of social skills. Turn-taking skills, for example, begin with a simple group task with the children working together to achieve the end result, and progress to the experience of taking part in a competitive game. Each activity has one main skill focus but may incorporate other skills previously met – for example, the 'Musical interlude' activity on page 24 focuses on working together as members of a group and includes the skills of sharing and turn-taking previously introduced.

Home links

Parents and carers should be actively encouraged to participate in all the activities in order to develop their children's social skills at home. Invite parents and carers into your setting to work alongside you, and regularly inform them of their children's progress and achievements. Use the 'Home links' suggestions to involve them in follow-up activities and discussions that will enhance their children's social development.

Mix and match

Learning objective
To concentrate and sit quietly when appropriate.

Group size
Four to six children

What you need
The photocopiable sheet; pairs of easily recognizable objects from around the setting, such as plastic cups, bricks, paintbrushes and small-world vehicles; scissors; card rectangles (approximately 17cm x 6cm); glue.

Preparation
Make two copies of the photocopiable sheet for each child.

What to do
Mix the objects on the floor and ask the children to look at them closely. Invite each child in turn to take two matching objects from the pile on

the floor. Talk about the difference between exact matches and things that are quite similar but vary, perhaps in colour or size.

Individual task
Give each child two copies of the photocopiable sheet. Ask them to point to an object on one sheet and then the matching object on the other. Show them how to cut out the pictures and stick them onto the card rectangles so that two pictures fit alongside each other to form a domino. Play a simple domino game with the children with each child using their own dominoes. Ask the children to take turns to place a domino on the table. The next child should join a domino with a matching picture to either end of the line of cards. If this is not possible, then the turn should be missed.

Support
Instead of making dominoes, create picture cards for the children. Play a simple matching game by placing the cards at random on the floor and mixing them up. Invite the children to pick up one card and then try to find another one with the same picture. If this is too easy, turn the cards upside-down and encourage the children to try to remember where they are.

Extension
Play commercial picture domino games of increasing difficulty and introduce more able children to traditional dominoes with spots.

Assessment
Record the children's concentration span and try to devise simpler, shorter tasks if they have difficulty in maintaining their interest, in order to develop this skill.

Home links
Let the children take their domino games home to play with their parents or carers and suggest that they play traditional dominoes together.

Mix and match

It's in the bag!

Learning objective
To be confident to try new activities, initiate ideas and speak in a familiar group.

Group size
Up to eight children.

What you need
The photocopiable sheet; selection of objects to match those on the photocopiable sheet; small bag; A4 card; scissors; glue.

Preparation
Copy the photocopiable sheet onto card and cut out the pictures to form a set of cards. Put these in the bag. Collect together objects resembling the pictures on the cards as closely as possible.

What to do
Invite the children to sit in a circle and spread the objects in front of them. Tell them that you are going to play a guessing game. Describe one of the objects and ask the children to point to it. Invite a child to pick up the object and hold it up. Encourage them to return it to the circle, then to describe another object for the rest of the children to guess. Continue until all the children have had a turn and are familiar with ways of describing the objects.

Individual task
Hold up the bag of cards and shake it in front of the children. Invite a confident child to begin the game by pulling a card out of the bag and describing it to the rest of the group without them seeing the card. Encourage the children to put up their hands if they think they know what is depicted on the card. Invite a child to say what is on the card and to put it next to the chosen object. Ask the other children if it is in the correct place. Continue until all children have had a turn.

Support
Put the picture cards on the floor and the objects in a larger bag. Invite a child to pull out an object, say what it is and put it beside the appropriate picture. Continue the matching game until all objects are out of the bag and put beside a matching picture.

Extension
Encourage the children to play the game as an 'I spy' activity.

Assessment
Note how confident the children are. Do they suggest ideas? Are they comfortable when they speak in front of the group? Plan further similar activities if they lack confidence.

Home links
Draw a selection of objects that can be found in the home on a sheet of paper so that the children can play the game with their parents or carers.

It's in the bag!

Fingers with feelings

Learning objective
To develop an awareness of their own needs, views and feelings and be sensitive to those of others in the group.

Group size
Four to six children

What you need
The photocopiable sheet; thin card; scissors; crayons or paints; paper; A4 card; sticky tape; flip chart; pen.

Preparation
Copy the photocopiable sheet onto thin card for each child.

What to do
Ask the children to think of times when they have felt sad or happy. Make a list of the children's thoughts on the flip chart and discuss any similarities. Now ask the children to think of situations where they have felt surprised or frightened. Invite each child to paint or draw a picture of a time when they have felt happy, sad, surprised or frightened. Use the children's drawings to create a book about feelings, writing what they say underneath each picture.

Individual task
Give each child a copy of the photocopiable sheet. Invite them to colour in the templates and to cut them out. Make a reversible finger puppet for each child by taping the happy and sad faces back to back with enough room for the puppet to fit on a child's finger. Repeat the exercise for the surprised and frightened faces. Help the children to put one of their puppets onto a finger on each hand. Look through the home-made book and talk about each picture. Ask the children to hold up the puppet that most fits the picture in the book. Have all the children chosen the same puppet? If not, why?

Support
Tell a simple story involving a sad event and a happy ending and ask the children to hold up the 'happy' or 'sad' face of their finger puppet at the appropriate time.

Extension
Create a puppet theatre from recycled boxes and encourage the children to make up their own stories using their puppets. Invite them to put on a show for the younger children.

Assessment
Record how confidently the children can talk about their feelings. Do they have difficulty talking about stronger emotions such as fear and grief? Carry out further activities relating to feelings sensitively for any children with emotional problems.

Home links
Invite parents and carers to come to your setting to watch their children perform their puppet shows at the 'puppet theatre'.

Skills for early years Social skills

Fingers with feelings

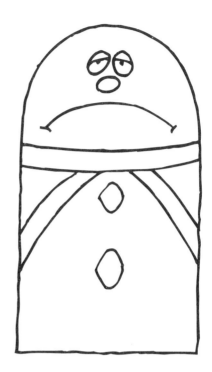

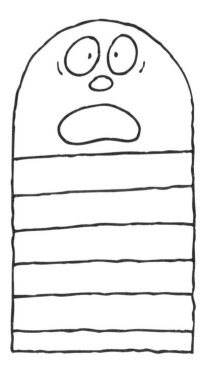

All buttoned up

Learning objective
To have a developing awareness of their own needs, views and feelings and be sensitive to the needs, views and feelings of others.

Group size
Four to six children

What you need
The photocopiable sheet; selection of four pairs of buttons varying in size, colour and brightness for each child; glue; crayons.

Preparation
Collect together a good selection of buttons and ensure that there are enough to create four easily distinguished matching groups. Make two copies of the photocopiable sheet for each child.

What to do
Ask the children to point to any buttons that they are wearing and talk about the different shapes, colours and sizes. Invite the children to look at your selection of mixed buttons and encourage each child to choose a favourite one, giving a reason for their choice.

Individual recording
Give each child two photocopiable sheets and four matching pairs of buttons, ensuring that the pairs vary in size, colour and brightness. Ask each child to look at the coats on both their photocopiable sheets and explain that one of the coats is going to be for themselves and the other is to be for a friend. Ask them to choose a friend and think about which buttons their friend might like on their coat. Then ask them to glue the buttons onto the coats, remembering that one of the coats is for themselves and the other is for a friend. Discuss with the children why they made their choices.

Support
Give the children two sets of four matching buttons and ask them to make sure that each coat has the same buttons. Help them with this if necessary.

Extension
Before sticking on the buttons, invite each child to colour in the coats using colours that they would like for themselves and colours that their chosen friend might like. Encourage them to work with a special friend in the group to complete this task.

Assessment
Observe how the children approach the activity. Do they consider sharing equally and making the two coats the same? Do they think about the views and feelings of their chosen friends or do they just consider their own feelings and stick the most attractive buttons to their own coats?

Home links
Ask parents and carers to encourage their families to consider the views and feelings of other family members by discussing preferences and making choices together at home, for example, at mealtimes and when out shopping.

All buttoned up

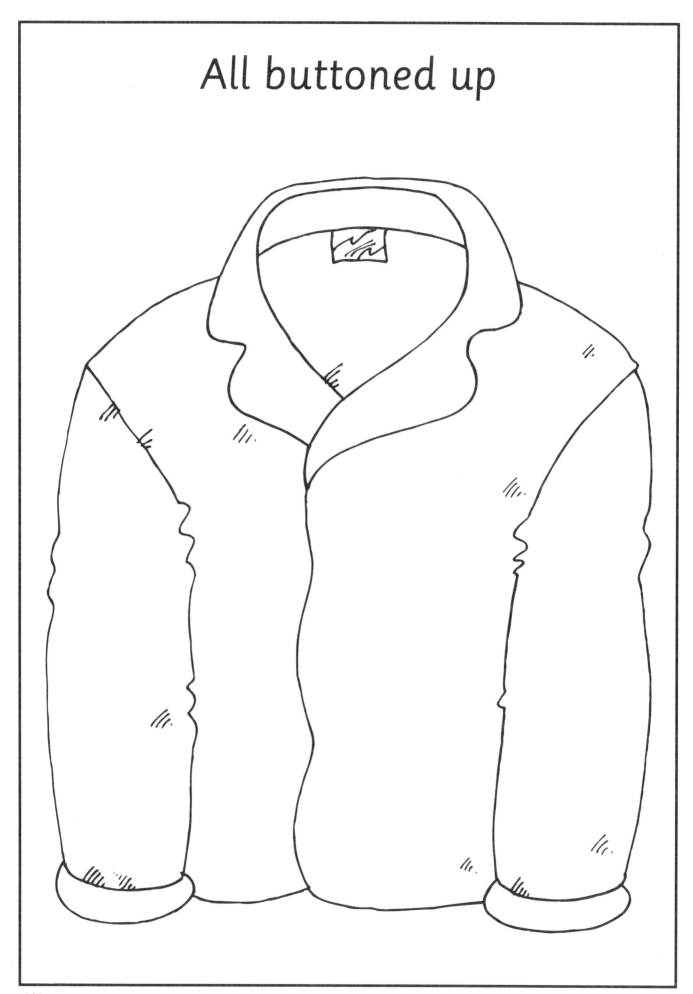

Teddy bears' picnic

Learning objective
To work as part of a group, taking turns and sharing fairly.

Group size
Four children.

What you need
The photocopiable sheet; scissors; glue; crayons; the children's teddies brought from home; eight pieces of A4 card.

Preparation
Ask each child to bring in two of their teddies from home. Make a copy of the photocopiable sheet for each child.

What to do
Talk to the children about their teddies and explain to them that they are going to make a picnic for their teddies. Encourage the group to set places for them in the home corner. Give each child two pieces of A4 card to represent the teddies' place mats and a copy of the photocopiable sheet. Look at the sheet together and point out the two plates and the strip of

pairs of items along the edge of the sheet. How do the children think that they can share out the items to make sure that their teddies all have the same picnic?

Individual recording
Invite the children to colour their place mats with a pattern of their choice, then to cut out the plate outlines and stick them onto the place mats that they have made. Encourage them to cut out the cups and napkins and stick them alongside the plates. The children can then cut out the pairs of food pictures and put one on each plate. Now look closely at the place settings together and see if all the teddies have the same picnic. If they are the same, the children can stick them on. If some are different, talk about why and what can be done to make them the same. When the children have finished, let them colour the place settings.

Support
If necessary, help the children with cutting out. Make sharing less confusing by cutting out the objects in pairs and letting the children put them on the plates straight away, rather than letting them cut them all out first.

Extension
Ask each child to write the names of their teddies on the place settings, and suggest that they cut a fringe along the edge of the place mat to decorate it. Cut out all the objects first and then share them.

Assessment
Observe whether the children understand the idea of sharing the objects equally, and add written comments to their finished place settings. Copy the place settings for their assessment files.

Home links
Ask parents and carers to introduce opportunities for their children to share things out at home, for example, by setting the table.

Teddy bears' picnic

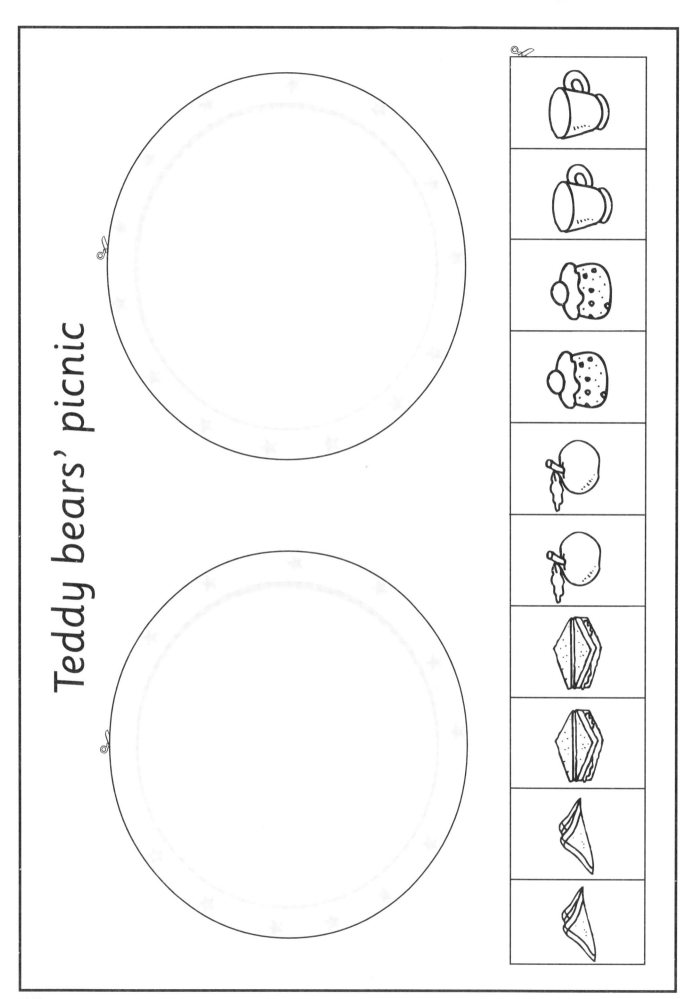

Sharing shapes

Learning objective
To work as part of a group, taking turns and sharing fairly.

Group size
Four to six children.

What you need
The photocopiable sheet; scissors; glue; card; selection of plastic shapes such as triangles, squares, rectangles and circles.

Preparation
Make a copy of the photocopiable sheet and cut a large circle of card for each child.

What to do
Show the children a pile of plastic triangles, squares, rectangles and circles of the same colour and size. Invite the children to share the shapes out so that they all have the same number of each shape. Ask them if they think it is easy to share the shapes equally. Give each child a copy of the photocopiable sheet. Invite the children in turn to point to a shape as you name it. Encourage them to count how many circles, squares, triangles and rectangles they have on their photocopiable sheets.

Individual recording
Give each child a disc of card and a pair of scissors and ask them to cut out the shapes from the photocopiable sheet. Now encourage them to sort their shapes into two groups so that they have a circle, a square, a triangle and a rectangle in each. Once everyone has divided the shapes equally, the children can stick them onto the disc of card. Ask the children to stick the matching shapes next to each other on the card.

Support
Give the children a pile of identical small objects such as plastic bears to share equally between them. Encourage them to take turns to pick up an object. When all the objects have gone, count how many each child has got. Have the objects been shared equally? How do the children know?

Extension
Ask the children to colour in the matching pairs of shapes in different colours before sticking them onto the card. Draw further shapes in spaces on the sheet such as a diamond or semicircle to extend the children's shape vocabulary and sharing skills

Assessment
Observe how easily the children sort the shapes into matching pairs. Have they understood the concept of sharing the shapes out equally? Copy the finished sheets for their assessment files along with comments about their verbal and active responses to the activity.

Home links
Encourage parents and carers to discuss shapes with their children at home and create simple sorting exercises using household objects.

Sharing shapes

All the way home

Learning objectives
To work as part of a group, taking turns and sharing fairly; to understand that there needs to be agreed values and codes of behaviour.

Group size
Four children.

What you need
The photocopiable sheet; A3 card; small plastic model dog; dice; small stickers.

Preparation
If possible, enlarge the photocopiable sheet and mount it onto A3 card to make a gameboard. Attach a sticker onto each face of a dice, marking three sides with the number '1' and the other three sides with the number '2'.

What to do
Ask the children to look at the gameboard and explain that the puppy has lost its mother. Talk about the journey that the puppy will have to make before it finds its mother. Tell the children that the puppy will have to go across a river, through the woods and past some houses. Ask the group to think of any dangers that the puppy may encounter. Does everyone think it would be a good idea to help the puppy find its mother?

Individual task
Encourage the children to work together to help the puppy cross the path to find its mother. Invite each child to roll the dice and move the small model puppy the correct number of spaces across the board. Emphasize to the children the importance of working together as a group to help the puppy.

Support
Draw spots on the dice stickers instead of numbers so that the children can move the puppy the corresponding number of spaces more easily.

Extension
Prepare the gameboard by colouring the squares numbered 2, 6 and 9 with a red felt-tipped pen. Explain to the children that the rules of the game are as follows: if the puppy lands on square 2, he could fall in the river; if he lands on square 6, he could get lost in the woods, and if he lands on square 9, he could get lost among the houses. Tell the children that if they land on one of these red squares, they will have to move back one space to avoid the danger and try to pass it on their next turn.

Assessment
Observe the children's enthusiasm when working as part of a team to help the puppy. Note whether they take turns willingly and follow the simple rules of the game.

Home links
Give each child a copy of the photocopiable sheet to take home to play the game with their parents and carers, making sure that they can explain the rules of the game to their carers!

 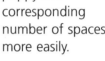

All the way home

The horse race

Learning objective
To work as part of a group, taking turns and sharing fairly.

Group size
Three children.

What you need
The photocopiable sheet; small spot stickers in three different colours; dice; sticky-backed plastic or a laminator.

Preparation
Cover each face of the dice with one of the three different-coloured spot stickers, making sure that the stickers on opposite sides of the dice are the same colour. Make a copy of the photocopiable sheet and cover it with sticky-backed plastic, or laminate it, for protection.

What to do
Show the children the gameboard on the photocopiable sheet and ask each child to choose a different-coloured spot sticker and place it beside one of the horse tracks on the board. Then ask each child to wear the same coloured sticker as a matching badge.

Individual task
Invite the children to take turns to throw the dice and explain that the child whose badge and sticker colour appears on the dice can add a sticker onto the next square on the track until one horse reaches the finish. The idea of the game is that the children work together to help a horse to win the race rather than compete against each other. Peel off the stickers at the end of the game, ready to start again.

Support
Place ten counters of three different colours into a small bag. Allow each child to take turns to pick out a counter and place it on the correct track until one horse reaches the finish.

Extension
Create a dice labelled with numbers 1, 2 and 3 on opposite sides. Use small plastic horses and ask each child to choose a track and horse. Invite the children to take turns to roll the dice and move their horses along the track the correct number of spaces.

Assessment
Observe the children's understanding about taking turns and working as a team rather than individually. Note whether they understand the simple rules of the game.

Home links
Explain to parents and carers that their children have been playing board games to encourage turn-taking, and ask them to play games involving taking turns at home.

The horse race

Start

Finish

Honey bears

Learning objective
To work as part of a group, taking turns and understanding that there needs to be agreed codes of behaviour to work together harmoniously.

Group size
Three children.

What you need
The photocopiable sheet; three small plastic bears of different colours; dice; spot stickers; felt-tipped pen; sticky-backed plastic or a laminator.

Preparation
Make a copy of the photocopiable sheet and cover it with sticky-backed plastic, or laminate it, for protection. Attach spot stickers to the faces of the dice and write the numbers 1, 2 and 3 on opposite faces.

What to do
This activity introduces the moral element of taking turns at the correct time and accepting that winning is not always inevitable. Talk about games that the children enjoy playing. Show them the photocopiable sheet and explain that the idea of this game is to move plastic bears across the squares, through the wood, to reach the jar of honey on the other side, by taking turns to roll the dice.

Individual task
Ask each child to choose a plastic bear and to take turns to roll the dice. Help the children to move their bears across the correct number of squares on the board. During the game, discuss the positions of the bears. Who is in the lead? How many squares are there between the first bear and the honey? When the winner reaches the honey, continue playing until everyone has finished. Talk about the results of the game. Who came second and third?

Support
Colour the sides of the dice the same colours as the bears. Invite the children to take turns to roll the dice. The player whose bear is the same colour as that shown on the dice must move on one space.

Extension
Number the squares and write instructions in some of the squares, for example, 'Miss a turn' or 'Move on 2 squares'.

Assessment
Do the children follow the simple rules? Are they aware of the reason why they need to take turns? Do they show pleasure when their friends win or just when they win themselves? Are they able to talk about their contrasting emotions when they win and when they lose?

Home links
Encourage parents and carers to play simple board games with their children at home.

Honey bears

Start

HONEY

Ring of friendship

Learning objective
To form good relationships with peers.

Group size
Six children.

What you need
The photocopiable sheet; card; scissors; glue; crayons; stapler (adult use); cotton.

Preparation
Cut strips of card approximately 60cm x 10cm. Make a copy of the photocopiable sheet for each child.

What to do
Talk to the children about the importance of friendship. Ask them who their friends are and why they like them. Encourage the children to link hands with their friends at your setting. Form a 'ring of friendship' with all the children by holding hands in a circle. Enjoy some favourite 'ring games' together such as 'Ring-o-Ring-o-Roses' and 'Hokey-cokey'.

Individual recording
Give each child a copy of the photocopiable sheet together with a strip of card and ask them to colour in the eight figures to represent their friends. Ask the children to cut out the boxes on the photocopiable sheet to make eight 'friends'. Remind them of the 'ring of friendship' and the 'ring games' that they played earlier and invite each child to make their own 'ring of friendship' by sticking the eight friends onto the strip of card with the hands touching. Bend each child's strip of card so that it forms a ring and secure it by stapling the two ends together. Suspend the 'rings' as mobiles from the ceiling at different heights using cotton tied at four equal intervals to the circle of card.

Support
Cut out the eight individual 'friend' pictures. Help the children to stick them onto the card making sure that all the hands are touching.

Extension
Ask each child to name seven 'friends' and help them to write each name on the figures. Ask them to write their own name on the eighth figure.

Assessment
Do the children understand what is meant by 'friend'? Can they name their friends? Write down their verbal comments about their choices.

Home links
Tell parents and carers about the activity. Give each child a copy of the photocopiable sheet to take home and ask parents and carers to create a 'ring of family friends' with their children.

Ring of friendship

Musical interlude

Learning objective
To work as part of a group, taking turns and sharing fairly.

Group size
Four children to make the badges; groups of up to 12 children to play the musical instruments.

What you need
The photocopiable sheet; card; scissors; glue; crayons; safety-pins; sticky tape; sticky-backed plastic; musical instruments – triangle, tambourine, drum and maracas (enough for one per child); screen or large sheet suspended across the room.

Preparation
Make the same number of copies of the photocopiable sheet onto card as there are musical instruments and children in the group.

What to do
Show the children the musical instruments and talk about what they are called. Pass around samples of each one and listen to the sounds that can be made. Familiarize the children with the sounds and names of the instruments by playing one behind a screen. Do the children recognize it by the sound?

Individual recording
Give each child a copy of the photocopiable sheet and ask them to colour in the instruments. Help them to cut out the circles. Cover these with sticky-backed plastic and attach safety-pins to the backs with sticky tape to create badges. Ask each child to choose a badge to wear and invite the group to sit in a circle. Place the instruments in a pile in the centre and invite the children to take turns to pick up the appropriate instrument according to the badge that they are wearing. Once the children have an instrument each, ask them to move into separate groups, one for each instrument. Sing appropriate songs together, such as 'I am a Music Man', 'Oh, We Can Play on the Big Bass Drum' and 'Here We Go Round the Mulberry Bush'. Encourage the children to play their instruments at the correct time.

Support
Let the children choose from two contrasting instruments and badges.

Extension
Dramatize a favourite story using the instruments to create sound effects. Make large pictures of the instruments to hold up and ask the children to play at the indicated time.

Assessment
Note whether the children understand the idea of working as a small group within a larger one.

Home links
Invite parents and carers to come to watch the children performing.

Musical interlude

Let's be kind

Learning objective
To understand what is right, what is wrong, and why.

Group size
Up to ten children.

What you need
The photocopiable sheet; crayons.

Preparation
Make a copy of the photocopiable sheet for each child.

What to do
Talk to the children about what they consider to be appropriate behaviour. Ask each child to think of a time when they have been friendly or helpful to someone when playing outdoors. Talk about ways of being friendly and helpful, such as helping to put on outdoor clothing, inviting others to join in a game or sharing toys. Ask the children if anyone has been unkind to them. Have they have ever been left out of a game or not been allowed to share toys with a friend? Can they explain how it feels?

Individual recording
Give each child a copy of the photocopiable sheet and discuss the scenes together. Encourage the children to choose an action and describe whether it is 'friendly' or 'unfriendly'. Ask the children to colour in the 'friendly' actions and to leave the 'unfriendly' actions as they are. Talk about the parts of the photocopiable sheet that the children have coloured in, inviting each child to explain why they made these choices. Has anybody coloured in an action that others consider to be 'unfriendly'? Can they explain why?

Support
Concentrate on using appropriate language rather than colouring the picture. Talk about the photocopiable sheet together. Point out a particular action and ask the children to tell you what is happening.

Extension
Encourage the children to be kind and helpful outdoors and to be sensitive to the needs of younger children. Dramatize the 'friendly' and 'unfriendly' actions on the photocopiable. Talk about how the children involved will be feeling. Act out an appropriate story, such as 'The Little Red Hen' (traditional), and emphasize the actions that are 'friendly' or 'unfriendly'.

Assessment
After the activity, monitor the children's behaviour outdoors and praise helpfulness. Observe whether they are beginning to recognize the differences between acceptable and unacceptable behaviour.

Home links
Ask parents and carers to encourage appropriate behaviour at home with their children, such as sharing toys and tidying up after play.

Let's be kind

Helping hands

Learning objective
To consider the consequences of their actions for themselves and others.

Group size
Four children

What you need
The photocopiable sheet; thick paint; shallow tray; crayons; Polaroid or digital camera.

Preparation
Make one copy of the photocopiable sheet for each child.

What to do
At the start of the session, tell the children that you are going to take some photographs of how they are being kind and helpful. Talk about the sort of shots you might be taking. At the end of the session, ask the children to talk about what they have been doing. Hold up your hands and ask the children to think about what their hands have been doing. Have any of the children done anything helpful with their hands, for example, shared a piece of equipment or helped to tidy things up? Tell the children about some of the photographs that you have taken and why you took them.

Individual recording
The following day, recall the previous discussion and suggest to the children that they might make a picture about their 'helping hands'. Give each child a copy of the photocopiable sheet

and help them to make a print of their own hand in the box at the bottom. Ask them to draw a picture of something helpful that they do for somebody else in each of the hand outlines at the top of the sheet.

Support
Show the children the photographs taken of their helpful or friendly actions such as tidying up, sharing equipment, holding hands with friends and hugging each other. Help each child to make a handprint in the box of their photocopiable sheet and ask them to use crayons to colour the hands at the top. Talk about the actions in the photographs and ask each child to try to do one of these during the session. Place their 'helping hands' picture beside the photograph and at the end of the session talk about whether they managed to complete their chosen action.

Extension
Help each child to write their name on their photocopiable sheet and encourage them to offer helping hands to younger children.

Assessment
Can the children look at the photographs and talk about the consequences of the actions that they see? Are they aware of the simple rules and expectations of the group?

Home links
Give each child a copy of the photocopiable sheet to take home to complete with their parents or carers drawings of 'helping hands' around the home.

Helping hands

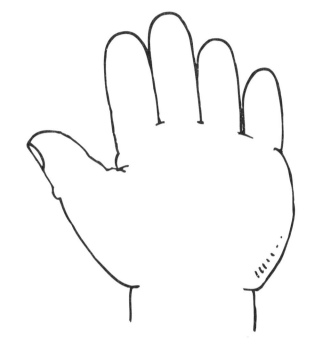 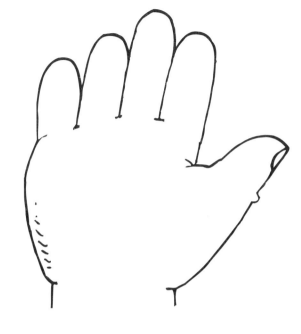

Name_____

Tidy-up time!

Learning objective
To understand that people have different needs that need to be treated with respect.

Group size
Up to ten children.

What you need
The photocopiable sheet; scissors; glue.

Preparation
Make a copy of the photocopiable sheet for each child. Involve the children in sweeping and mopping-up activities and encourage them to take an active part in 'tidy-up time'.

What to do
Discuss with the children how everyone is responsible for looking after the equipment and for tidying things away after use so that they are ready for others to use again. Encourage the children to consider the consequences of their actions, for example, what would happen if they left books on the floor or sticky marks on the table? Ask each child how they would feel if they went to play with something and discovered that somebody else had not put it back after using it.

Individual recording
Give each child a copy of the photocopiable sheet and talk about each of the four activities. Ask the children to describe each picture individually. Can they think of ways they might help to clear up the mess? Talk about the objects related to cleaning and tidying that are along the bottom of the photocopiable sheet. Discuss with the children which object would be most appropriate for clearing up the mess in each picture. What would happen if they used a mop to clear up bricks? Could they use the brick box to help clear up spilled sand? Ask each child to cut out each cleaning object and stick it beside the scene that they feel is most appropriate.

Support
Help the children to cut out the four cleaning objects and encourage them to choose the correct scenes through discussion.

Extension
Involve the children in trying out different ways of signalling to other children that it is 'tidy-up time', for example, walking around beating a drum, singing a favourite song, or putting on some taped music. Allocate responsibilities using a picture card system.

Assessment
Observe any changes in the children's behaviour after the activity. Are they sharing responsibility within the community?

Home links
Ask parents and carers to involve their children more in cleaning and tidying activities around the home.

Tidy-up time!

Name _____

Skills development chart

I can concentrate and sit quietly when I need to

I am confident to try new activities and suggest my own ideas

I am happy to take turns

I am becoming aware of my own needs, views and feelings

I consider the needs, views and feelings of others in the group

I can talk about my own feelings to another person

I am beginning to make friends

I have special friends I choose to play with

I can work as a member of a group

I can share a selection of objects fairly between two people

I consider the consequences of my words and actions on myself and others

I can relate to members of my own group during an activity

I am beginning to understand what is right and wrong, and why

I can speak in a familiar group with confidence

I understand how to follow simple rules and codes of behaviour of my group

I understand that people have different needs that need to be treated with respect

I am beginning to understand that I am a member of a community

📖 SCHOLASTIC

Skills for early years Social skills